MALE SPORTS STARS

IN THIS SERIES

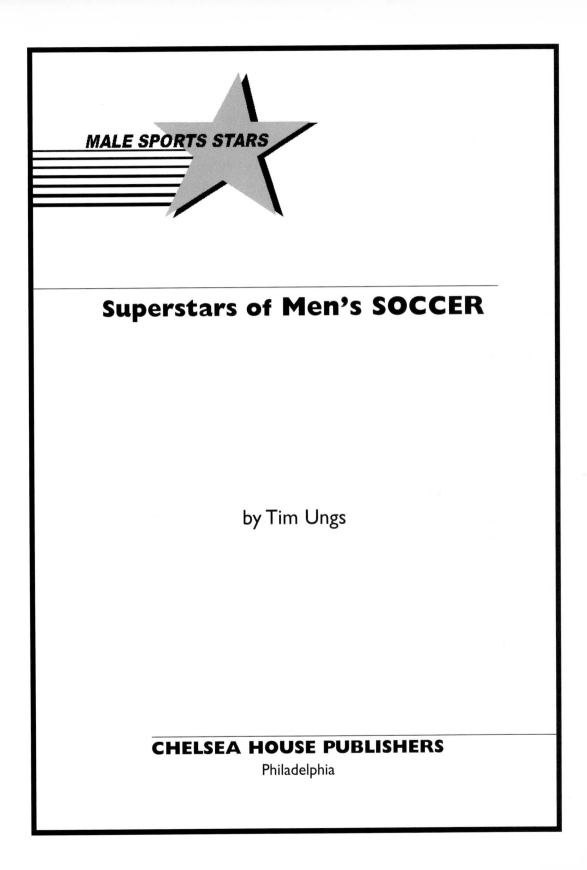

MALE SPORTS STARS

Superstars of Men's SOCCER

by Tim Ungs

CHELSEA HOUSE PUBLISHERS

Philadelphia

Designed by Combined Publishing
Conshohocken, Pennsylvania
Cover Illustration by Earl Parker

First Printing

1 3 5 7 9 8 6 4 2

Library of Congress Cataloging-in-Publication Data

Ungs, Tim
    Superstars of men's soccer / by Timothy Ungs.
        p.   cm.—(Male sports stars)
    Includes bibliographical references (p. 63) and index.
    Summary: Provides a brief look at some of the major players in
    men's soccer from its beginnings in the late 1800s to the 1990s,
    emphasizing the sport's relatively recent popularity in the United
    States.
        ISBN 0-7910-4588-9
        1.   Soccer—History—Juvenile literature.   2. Soccer Players—
    Biography—Juvenile literature.   [1. Soccer players.]   I. Title.
    II. Series.
    GV943.25.U54   1998
    796.334'092'2—dc21
                                                                                    97-50128
                                                                                        CIP
                                                                                          AC

CONTENTS

1

SOCCER BLOSSOMS IN AMERICA

From its origins in England in the 1860s, the game of soccer has spread, taken root, and been wildly embraced in every corner of the globe. Everywhere, that is, except the United States.

Gather together 10 soccer fans, and you'll get 10 different reasons for why this is so. But prior to the summer of 1994, at least, it was an indisputable fact—the world is crazy about soccer. Americans like baseball and football.

All that changed, many said, on July 4, 1988. FIFA, the World Soccer Federation, announced the United States would be the host country for the 1994 World Cup, the tournament held every four years to decide the world's best soccer team.

Beginning on June 17, 1994, the 24-team tournament, billed as "the biggest and most spectacular sporting event on earth," would be held in stadiums across America—in Boston, Chicago, Dallas, Detroit, Los Angeles, New York, Orlando, San Francisco, and Washington, D.C. More than a million foreign visitors would travel to the U.S. to watch the games, and billions more would be watching on television.

Not everyone welcomed the decision to stage the Cup in the States. Some soccer purists around the world were up in arms. There's no soccer tradition in America, they said. No one knows anything about soccer there, and worse, no one really cares.

U.S. soccer player Cle Klooman maneuvers past Swiss player Ciriacs Sforza in the 1994 World Cup series held for the first time ever in the United States.

There were grains of truth in this argument. An opinion poll taken virtually on the eve of the tournament revealed that only 20% of the American public knew the world championship of soccer was about to be held on American soil. And soccer certainly lacked the fan base of baseball, football, and basketball. On the other hand, no one could dispute that the game had a foothold in the U.S. In 1994, more than 16 million Americans said they played the game. Three million played at least once a week on average, and about the same number claimed soccer as their favorite sport. Among the young, especially, the game was enjoying spectacular growth. For boys and girls under 18, it was the third most popular sport (after basketball and volleyball), and among participants under 12, soccer trailed only basketball in popularity.

The history of the game in the U.S., while nowhere near as glorious as the history of British, Brazilian, Italian, or German soccer, does have some high (and low) points. Prior to June 21, 1994, there were some notable dates in U.S. soccer history, but not many.

* On June 29, 1950, the U.S. national team defeated England in a World Cup match in Belo Horizonte, Brazil. It was such a monumental upset that English journalists couldn't believe the score coming off the wire services in their offices. One soccer writer simply assumed it was a mistake. He amended the 1-0 score to read England 10, U.S.A. 0, a result more in line with what was expected. "This is all we needed to make the game go in the States," lamented England's coach, Bill Jeffery. He was wrong. No one noticed.

* On June 19, 1975, Pelé agreed to come to America to play for the New York Cosmos in the North American Soccer League. If anyone could make soccer a true major league sport in America, it was Pelé, the greatest player in the world and the man who led Brazil to three World Championships in four attempts.

By the end of the 70s, the NASL had a national TV contract and sex appeal. Mick Jagger, Rod Stewart, and Henry Kissinger could often be seen in the Cosmos locker room. Pelé was joined in America by such great, if fading, superstars as Johann Cruyff, Franz Beckenbauer, George Best, and Giorgio Chinaglia. For a while, it looked like soccer had a fighting chance. But 10 years after the arrival of Pelé, the Cosmos were the last—the only—NASL team left. On Father's Day 1985, they played a final exhibition match against Lazio, an Italian club team, in New York. Nine thousand fans stretched out in the 70,000-seat Giants Stadium. The NASL's swan song was marred by an all-out brawl on the field. "The outlook isn't bright," said Chinaglia, in something of an understatement. Professional soccer was dead in America and wouldn't be revived for another decade.

* On November 19, 1989, the United States needed to beat tiny Trinidad and Tobago to qualify for the 1990 World Cup, something they had not done in 40 years. Win they did, in dramatic fashion, on a clutch 35-yard curling shot by midfielder Paul Caligiuri. Some U.S. sportswriters hailed it as "the shot heard round the world." But as Pete Davies, a British soccer writer, put it, "the truth is that, around the world, we weren't listening." To the rest of the

Fans of the U.S. soccer team cheer their team in a first round World Cup soccer match in 1994.

U.S. soccer players react after a first half goal in the game against Trinidad that advanced them to the 1990 World Cup in Italy.

world, qualifying for the Cup was a big achievement for the Americans, but hardly ground-breaking news. The U.S. traveled to Italy for the 1990 tournament and lost badly to Czechoslovakia 5-1, to Italy 1-0, and to Austria 2-1. Two goals for, eight against. All they had to show for their effort was a moral victory for their scrappy play against the mighty Italians in front of a home crowd. The Americans "ran their hearts out," wrote Davies. "It wasn't always pretty but it was brave, and with a different roll of the ball it might have ended 1-1. The Italians were mightily embarrassed; the Americans were quietly proud."

Only six players from the team that played in Italy in 1990 were still around for the 1994 Cup: goalkeeper Tony Meola, defenders Paul Caligiuri and Marcelo Balboa, midfielders John Harkes and Tab Ramos, and forward Eric Wynalda. The team had a new coach in Bora Milutinovic, a Yugoslavian Serb who gained his reputation as a miracle worker by coaching first Mexico and then Costa Rica to impressive showings in the previous two World Cups. Bora spoke four languages—English was not one of them. But he came highly recommended by no less an authority than soccer legend Franz Beckenbauer. Milutinovic revamped the team's approach, throwing out the longball game of his predecessor Bob Gansler which emphasized size, speed, and strength. Instead he stressed a possession and control style, the more skills-based game generally associated with Latin American soccer. The American team played an ambitious series of exhibition matches against international competition and hosted two U.S. Cups in 1992 and 1993. At times, they held their own against some of the world's best teams.

But 1994 would be different. For the Americans in "their" World Cup, just looking good would no longer be enough.

Alan Rothenburg, the United States Soccer Federation president, may have been putting it too dramatically when he said, "The 1994 World Cup is the last chance for soccer in the United States," but the stakes were indeed high. The pressure on the players, great to begin with, was made even greater by the fact that MLS, the new national pro soccer league, would not be in place the day the Cup ended, as had been hoped.

The basic structure of the tournament was relatively simple. The 24 teams in the tournament were divided into six groups of four. A win in the first round was worth three points, a tie was worth one. The rule of thumb was that a team needed at least four points to go through to the next round, where single-elimination "knockout" play began.

"Much of the American interest will likely depend on the performance of the young, inexperienced U.S. team, which as the host automatically qualified for the tournament," wrote Jere Longman in the *New York Times*. In 60 years of World Cup competition, no host country had ever failed to advance to the second round, and the Americans had no desire to be the first to achieve that dubious distinction. Not having won a Cup match since they beat the British in 1950, the U.S. had to come up with something more than a moral victory in their opening round. The U.S. needed a win and a tie to go on to the next round.

America's group, Group A, wasn't the toughest in the tournament, but it was far from the easiest. Switzerland hadn't been to the finals since 1966, but they were a steady team, and they had Stephane Chapusiat, a scoring star for Borussia Dortmund in the Bundesliga, the top German league. The Swiss had had some impressive moments in qualifying, including a win and a tie against the always strong Italians. Romania, thought by many to be dangerous and underrated, because of its counterattacking style, were led by Gheorghe Hagi, crafty and creative in midfield, and boasted dangerous forwards Florin Raducioiu and Ilie Dumitrescu. And Colombia was picked by a straw poll of international journalists—and by Pelé himself—as a dark horse contender to win the entire tournament. Their captain, Carlos Valderrama, was impossible to miss, as much for his gigantic mass of frizzy blond hair as for the way he and his midfield partner Freddy Rincon controlled the flow of the game. They had a lethal scoring threat in Faustino Asprilla, a major force in Italian soccer, and had conquered Argentina twice in qualifying, including a dominating 5-0 victory—an incredible score, considering the match was played in front of a partisan Argentine crowd in Buenos Aires. Colombia was a team to be reckoned with.

The U.S. team's first match in Detroit ended in a 1-1 tie with Switzerland. The result was not a disaster, but it was a major disappointment. One point was better than none, but to advance the U.S. needed to win at least one of the three matches. If they couldn't do it against the Swiss, they'd have to do it against one of the two best teams in their group. By drawing instead of winning in the opener, they made the following match against a hungry Colombia—themselves surprise 3-1 losers to the Romanians—as close to a do-or-die match as an American team had ever faced.

On June 22, more than 93,000 spectators packed the Rose Bowl in Pasadena, California, to witness what was, in retrospect, the finest moment in the history of American soccer. The Americans were nervous before the match. "Obviously," said Tab Ramos, "the Colombians are the better team on paper. We can't match up with them man for man."

Alexi Lalas described the necessary strategy for the game. "We knew they would come down the middle of the field, and we knew we had to stifle them, frustrate them, and look for counterattacks." His analysis was on the money. The Colombians charged early and gave the U.S. a scare in the seventh minute. Herman Gaviria, off a pass from Freddy Rincon, had gotten past Tony Meola charging out of the goal, but was tackled from behind by Mike Sorber, who sent the ball straight towards the empty net—and into the left post. The Americans had barely managed to escape an embarrassing "own goal."

Twenty minutes later, the Colombians would not be so lucky. U.S. midfielder John Harkes broke down the left wing and sent a hard ball across the ground, intended for the swift Ernie Stewart. Colombian defender Andres Escobar raced back and slid to deflect the ball but instead knocked it past his own goalkeeper Oscar Cordoba and into the net. The crowd was at first stunned, then ecstatic. A little lucky surely, but a 1-0 lead nonetheless. The Americans carried that lead into the intermission.

Luck had nothing to do with it when, just a few minutes into the second half, Stewart took a chipped pass from Ramos, beat Escobar, then Cordoba, and booted the ball into the right corner of the goal. What the Americans dared only dream was becoming reality. They now led 2-0. A major upset was in the making, and in-the-know soccer people were beginning to realize the U.S. side was for real. Andres Cantor, the Spanish-language television announcer who became a World Cup celebrity with his emotional outbursts every time a goal was scored, praised Stewart's goal as one of the two most memorable of the tournament. Describing his now-famous call of the goal he wrote, "The scream started in my throat, and, five seconds later, disappeared into the air, overtaken by hoarseness. Instantaneously and instinctively, the 'Goooal!' I had started and lost burst out from the depths of my body. It was a bit more than the end of a hard day's work: It was the qualifying goal of the only team who could inspire those who believed soccer was boring and useless."

The U.S. had one of the pre-tournament favorites down two goals and only had to hang on for the victory. Defenders Lalas, Marcelo Balboa, Caligiuri, and Fernando Clavijo stopped the Colombians' charge up the middle of the field and continued to press the attack. The Colombians got a goal back late in the match, but it was too little, too late. And to cap off a terrific showing, a spectacular match highlight came in the closing minutes when Balboa barely missed a dramatic backwards-somersaulting bicycle kick. Had that shot gone in, wrote one spectator, "the entire country might have died a soccer death, stricken by overexcitement." The

United States forward Ernie Stewart, second from left, joins teammates Tab Ramos (9) and Thomas Dooley, left, to celebrate Stewart's goal during the 1994 World Cup Soccer championship Group A first round match at the Rose Bowl in Pasadena, Calif., June 22, 1994.

Americans not only had beaten a top team, they had done so with some style. Outshot in the match 14-7, they nonetheless controlled play from the opening minutes.

Lalas, who with his spirited play, goatee, and wild mane of red hair (one reporter likened him to "a heavy metal Ronald McDonald") became another of the Cup's instant celebrities. "It's incredible, it's historical, it's very cool," he said. "We were the only ones who thought it was possible." Lalas insisted, however, that the match was not, as some described it, a miracle. "A miracle," he said, putting things into perspective, "is when a baby survives a plane crash."

A few days later, in a horrifying turn of events, still more perspective was put on the match. Andres Escobar, whose mistake gave the Americans their early lead, returned to Colombia and was brutally murdered by thugs in Medellin who faulted him for the team's defeat. It was a grim reminder that the world's great passion for the game of soccer has its dark side, too.

It's possible that the extended celebration after the victory made it difficult for the Americans to focus their attention on their next match with Romania. Or it might have been the 120-degree heat on the field at game time. Whatever the cause, they were beaten by the Romanians the following Sunday, June 26. The Romanians were the surprise winners of Group A, but the Americans, with a win and a tie, had enough to go through to the second round. They had accomplished what they set out to do, and in the process were winning the respect of the soccer world. The ultimate test lay ahead: mighty Brazil was to be their opponent on the Fourth of July.

The Independence Day match was played in Stanford Stadium, just outside of San Francisco. The Americans frustrated Romario, Bebeto, Rai, Dunga, Branco, and the rest of the powerful Brazilian squad throughout the game, but they were outshot 16-4, and none of their four shots was on goal. An early chance by midfielder Thomas Dooley in the 12th minute was as close as they got to scoring. But there was no denying that their pesky defensive effort got under the skin of the Brazilians. Mazinho and Jorginho drew yellow cards in the early going, and a minute from half-time Leonardo was ejected for his vicious elbow to the head of Tab Ramos (a blow that caused a concussion and kept the American star off the soccer field for six months). Forced to play a man short, the Brazilians nevertheless kept pressuring the American goal and, finally, 74 minutes into the game, Romario saw an opening and slid a perfect pass to Bebeto, who shot it home. It was all the Brazilians needed.

After the match, 84,147 fans chanted "U-S-A! U-S-A!" and Brazilian players displayed the Stars and Stripes in the center of the field. The Americans were, of course, saddened by the defeat, but knew they could be proud of their effort. U.S. assistant coach Timo Liekoski acknowledged that he had gotten his hopes up when the U.S. turned back the Brazilian attack time after time. "When they failed to convert a couple of their chances, it seemed someone was looking out for us," he told the *New York Times*. "But it wasn't meant to be.

Brazilian player Bebeto (7) in action during the second round of the World Cup Soccer match July 4, 1994. Brazil won the match against the U.S. team, 1-0.

Maybe someone's telling us, keep working and it will come."

Marcelo Balboa, the defender who was making the last of his record 94 appearances for the United States, said, "We gave everything we could on the field . . . . People who knew nothing of soccer now understand the passion that sport brings." And he was right. The rest of America's World Cup was a resounding success—the most successful Cup ever, in fact, and the American audience eagerly joined in with the rest of the world in following the action. On July 17, the final match with Brazil defeating Italy drew 94,194 fans. Net gate receipts totaled $43.5 million, reportedly a record for any single sporting event anywhere.

The record average attendance at the matches was 68,102, which shattered the previous record of 48,411.

But this World Cup's greatest success could not be measured in dollars or attendance numbers. America's players had played well, and their fans had embraced the game. The U.S. had been brought into the fold. "The atmosphere in the stadiums has been fantastic," Paul Gardner, author of the classic *The Simplest Game*, told *World Soccer* magazine. "You could be in Rio or Milan or anywhere. There's been a lot of cheering, a lot of excitement and passion inside the stadiums and around them. The party atmosphere has been terrific." It had taken a long time, but in 1994, America experienced soccer's excitement firsthand, and finally understood why Pelé called it "the beautiful game."

2

PELÉ

At the 1958 World Cup Finals, Brazil was among the 16 soccer powers that gathered in Sweden to do battle for the Jules Rimet Trophy, awarded every four years since 1930 to the world's best national soccer team.

At the time, Brazil was known for playing an entertaining but frustratingly ineffective brand of soccer. They were highly skilled, always attacked, and were fun to watch—but they never came through when it counted. In 1950, Brazil had been on the losing end of what was perhaps the biggest upset in soccer history when, playing at home in front of 200,000 fans in Rio de Janeiro's Maracana Stadium, they fell to neighbor and bitter rival Uruguay. Four years later in Switzerland, they were eliminated in the quarterfinals by Hungary, and some of their players vented their frustrations in a brutal postgame brawl—the match came to be known as the Battle of Berne.

The Brazilian national team had gone home losers each time they appeared in previous World Cups, and the 1958 competition got off to a shaky start. In their first two games, Brazil squeaked by Austria 1-0 and played England to a scoreless draw. Three team leaders, Bellini, Didi, and Nilton Santos suggested—some say demanded—a number of lineup changes. Brazil's coach Vicente Feola listened and took Altafina and Dino Sani out of the starting line-

Pelé heads the ball past the New York Cosmos goalie during his final game at Giants Stadium. Pelé is soccer's most famous superstar.

up, replacing them with Zito and Vava. Garrincha was inserted into the starting lineup at right wing. And a forward called Pelé, just 17 at the time, would don the verdeamarelha, Brazil's famous green and yellow jersey, for the first time against the Soviet Union.

The results of Feola's changes were immediate and spectacular. Brazil beat the Soviets so handily that after the game the Russian coach was moved to say, "I can't believe what we saw this afternoon was soccer. I have never seen anything so beautiful in my life." At the center of their attack was a remarkably mature Pelé. The young star didn't score in his first game against the Soviets, but he got his first World Cup goal 66 minutes into his second. The game was a tightly contested quarterfinal match against Wales, and the goal was crucial. It held up as the only score, and it put Brazil through to the next round, a highly anticipated contest with France.

Prior to the semifinals, Pelé's play had been impressive, but in the match against France he made it clear that he was truly a sensational player. French scoring ace Juste Fontaine was the toast of the tournament with eight goals in the first four games (he would end up with 13 for the tournament, a record that still stands), and he wasted no time in getting France onto the scoreboard, scoring in the ninth minute to tie the game after an early Brazilian strike. But late in the first half, a French player was badly injured. Because no substitutions were allowed at the time, the French were forced to play a man down. 10 French players were no match for 11 Brazilians (in fact, after the game their goalkeeper, Claude Abbes, made the famous declaration, "I would rather play against ten Germans than one Brazilian"). One 17-year-old Brazilian, in particular, proved to be the worst thorn in Abbes' side. Pelé scored a hat trick—three goals—in the second half of the semifinal.

Pelé still fondly and vividly remembers June 28, 1958, the day of the championship game against Sweden, the tournament's host. "Seventeen years old, imagine that!" he told Andres Cantor. "What comes to mind—and it's almost as if I could hear it now—is the national anthem of my country playing, and me surrounded by foreigners. I don't know, but it occurs to me now that someone must have asked himself: 'What's that kid doing there in the midst of so many giants?'"

If he—or anyone—had doubts that he belonged, those doubts were quickly put to rest. Brazil was down a goal just three minutes into the game, but Vava, off a beautiful feed from Garrincha, equalized the score at nine minutes. From there they dominated play, going on to win 5-2. Pelé had two of Brazil's goals (giving him six in four games), both beauties. He put the exclamation point on the victory with a gravity-defying header in the final minutes, and dazzled everyone with a goal for the ages early in the second half. Amid traffic in the penalty area in front of the Swedish goal, Pelé got in position to bring in a high pass. He controlled it with his thigh, tapped it nonchalantly over the head of a dumbfounded defender, then turned and hammered a volleying shot into the net, just inside the post.

Brazil rejoiced in its victory, and many in Stockholm's Rasunda Stadium, caught up by the South Americans' exciting style of play, rejoiced with them. "There was no doubt this time that the best, immeasurably the finest team had won," wrote Brian Glanville in his book, *The Story of the World Cup.* Sweden 1958 was the coming-out party for the Brazilians, the beginning of their remarkable run of three world championships in four tries. And it was a sparkling debut for the teenage sensation who would go on to become a household name.

Born into humble circumstances in 1940, Pelé was baptized Edson Arantes do Nascimento, a name inspired by Thomas Edison, his father said. What inspired his nickname no one knew, not even Pelé himself. He does remember hating it and getting in fights at school when other kids would call him Pelé. His family was poor; he worked as a shoeshine boy to supplement his family's income and became a cobbler's apprentice for a while. But his real love was soccer. He played in the streets with a ball made of old socks and was tutored by his father, who had been a good player in his day— like so many Brazilian players, he went by a single nickname, Donadinho—but had his career shortened by injuries.

Pelé's rise to the top of the soccer world was meteoric. At 15, he was signed by the Brazilian club team Santos—and he played for no other club for the next quarter of a century. It didn't take long for him to make an impression. At first he "was just an errand boy for the older players," said his Santos coach. "Then, before they knew it, they were looking up to him." At 16, he was called up to the international team.

At 5' 8" and 150 pounds, Pelé was stocky and muscular. He was a brilliant juggler and dribbler, had a powerful right-footed shot, and seemed to have no limit on his vertical leap. Like a young Michael Jordan, Pelé simply jumped as high as he needed to go. Yet his physical attributes told only part of the story. "Above all," wrote Brian Glanville, "his temperament was extraordinary, his coolness in the thick of battle, the most tense and dramatic situations, uncanny." Like all the great players, his genius was a combination of physical gift, vision, determination, and creativity. Brazil absolutely loved him and wouldn't hear of him playing anywhere else. When there were rumors about an Italian club team trying to lure Pelé to play in Europe, the government even stepped in and declared him a "national treasure"—meaning he could not be exported!

Pelé led Santos to Brazilian championships five times. Santos also won both the South American Club Cup and the World Club Cup in 1962 and 1963.

At the 1962 World Cup in Chile, Brazil won the Rimet Trophy once again. Pelé, at his peak at 21 and now considered the world's best player, played brilliantly in the opener against Mexico, beating four defenders and the goalkeeper with a mighty shot to score one goal and setting up another. But he injured his thigh in the second match and had the bittersweet experience of cheering his team on from the sidelines as they rolled over Czechoslovakia 3-1 in the final match in Santiago.

The 1966 tournament in England was even more frustrating: it was the only World Cup in which Pelé played on a losing side. As in the

Pelé flies through the air as he kicks the ball back over his head. Pelé was a talented dribbler as well as shot–maker.

previous Cup, injuries bothered Pelé, but the real problem was the vicious treatment he was getting at the hands—and feet—of opposing defenders. He had become a marked man. In Brazil's final first-round match against Portugal he was brought down by a particularly vicious tackle. Bitter about his team's elimination and his mistreatment, Pelé vowed never to take part in another World Cup.

Fortunately for Brazil and for world soccer, he changed his mind four years later when Mexico hosted the 1970 tournament. After a pre-tournament controversy in which Brazil's coach actually contemplated dropping Pelé from the national team—the coach was fired instead—Brazil took the field with a potentially counterproductive collection of players. The new coach, Mario Lobo Zagallo, a former team-

Pelé, right, shown playing for Brazil's Santos Soccer Team in the U.S. Cup match in August 1966. Two U.S. professional soccer leagues were announced at the match, one of which would eventually draw Pelé away from his Brazilian team.

mate of Pelé's, went with Tostao, Jairzinho, Gerson, Roberto Rivelino, and Pelé. Some criticized his decision, saying those five superstars played overlapping roles.

As they had done 12 years earlier, however, the Brazilian players took matters into their own hands. Realizing the potential difficulty, they held a team meeting and agreed that unity was to be foremost in everyone's mind. As it turned out, there was no need to worry. The Brazilian team scored at least three goals in every game except one—a tough battle versus defending champion England—and drew praise from all quarters for their spirited, innovative, attacking style of play.

The final game versus Italy was a symbolic clash between two styles of play. The Italians had developed and were masters of catenaccio. Literally "a great chain," the catenaccio game stressed defense above everything: the idea was to score early on the counterattack, then pack defenders around the goal and hope to win a low-scoring contest. It was effective but not especially pretty to watch. It was playing not to lose. The Brazilians played a purer, more entertaining brand of soccer. The final match, wrote Paul Gardner, came down to "soccer's version of the Forces of Light versus the Forces of Darkness."

And the Forces of Light came out on top. Making a mockery of Italy's cynical defensive stance, Brazil ran rampant, winning 4-1. Pelé was without doubt the man of the match, setting up two goals beautifully and scoring on a header that Andres Cantor describes as "the ultimate triumph of pure artistry." It came early in the match. Rivelino lofted a fairly ordinary-looking pass into the goal mouth; the tall Italian defenders leapt to head it away, but Pelé exploded above them, twisted his body in midair, and headed the ball past Enrico Albertosi, the Italian goalkeeper. It was the first goal he had scored in a World Cup final since his debut a dozen years earlier, and it was strikingly similar to his coup de grace of the Swedish competition.

The 1970 World Cup was broadcast live worldwide—even in the United States—and soccer fans around the globe would forever remember the Brazilian celebration afterwards (the Italians, as had become a sad custom, went home to an airport reception of rotten

Pelé and Cosmos teammate John Kerr (6) congratulate each other after Pelé made an assist in his debut game with the New York team in 1975. He piloted the Cosmos to a 2-2 tie.

fruit and insults). Fans hoisted the bare-chested Brazilian players onto their shoulders and danced around the field. "In this exuberance, this unconfined delight," wrote Brian Glanville, "one seemed to see a reflection of the way Brazil had played; and played was, indeed, the word. For all their dedication, all their passion, they and their country had somehow managed to remain aware that football was, after all, a game; something to be enjoyed." This victory had special significance for the Brazilians. As three-time winners of the Cup, they became permanent holders of the Jules Rimet Trophy. The next competition would be played for a new trophy called the FIFA Cup. It was appropriate that this end to an era coincided with Pelé's exit from the World Cup.

In 1975, Pelé came to play in America. As the highly-paid star of the New York Cosmos, he was still in the spotlight, still a hero to millions. But for most of the '70s, he was more of an ambassador for the sport than a force as a player. (Alan Rothenberg called him "the single most important person in bringing the World Cup to the United States.") The Cosmos didn't win the "Soccer Bowl" in 1975 or 1976, but with the arrival of Franz Beckenbauer in 1977—Pelé's last year of playing—they broke through and took the championship.

Pelé continues to be a major supporter of soccer around the world. After Pelé, the game would never be the same.

Fans swarm onto the field during the World Soccer Cup in 1970 in Mexico. Pelé had just led Brazil to a 4-1 defeat of Italy in the title match. Ecstatic rooters tore the shirts off the victors and carried Pelé around the field.

BRILLIANT PLAYERS WITH A BALL

3

After Pelé's retirement, the best soccer players in the world were unquestionably Franz Beckenbauer, a West German, and Johann Cruyff, a Dutchman. The only two players ever named European Footballer of the Year three times, they were both magnificent, supremely intelligent tacticians on the field. Both were great team leaders—for their national and club teams alike—and both associated with what has come to be known as the Total Soccer style of play. In a fitting high point to each of their careers, they met head to head in Munich in 1974, in one of the most memorable World Cup finals in history.

The first of these players, Franz Beckenbauer, was born in Munich in the hard months immediately following the end of World War II. As a youth, he briefly considered a career in medicine and became an insurance salesman trainee before realizing his future lay with the game the Germans call *futbol*. He joined his first team at the age of 10, and a few years later was playing with the youth division of the Bayern Football Club.

Compared to Pelé, he was a late bloomer, for he was 19 when he first played for the senior team in 1964. His progress from that point on, however, was rapid and dramatic. In 1965, he was chosen for the West German national team and made his first appearance for his country in

The Cosmos' Franz Beckenbauer (6) and Pelé during a game in Portland with Seattle. After Pelé retired, Beckenbauer emerged as one of soccer's best players.

a World Cup qualifying match against Sweden. The next year, he led Bayern to the German Cup championship in the club's first season in the Bundesliga and made an impressive debut in the 1966 World Cup as an attacking midfielder. The Germans finished second to the host country England, beaten in the final game by a "phantom goal" in extra time that, replays later showed, never actually crossed the goal line.

After that painful loss, Beckenbauer turned his attention to his club team, and with the support of Bayern's coach, Tschik Cajovski, he began to experiment with his position on the field. The raw material for his experimentation was the often effective but invariably dull catenaccio, then a prevalent formation, especially in the Italian league. Catenaccio used four fullbacks at the back of the defense. Three of these were given specific area assignments; the fourth, known as the libero or "sweeper," played behind the other three. In catenaccio, the libero's responsibility was mainly defensive. The equivalent of a free safety in football, his job was to plug any gaps left open by the other defenders.

A student of the game, Beckenbauer had long been impressed by how dangerous on offense the great Italian defender Giacinto Fachetti had been for Inter Milan. Fachetti scored 60 goals in an 18-year career, an amazing total for a fullback. Beckenbauer thought what Fachetti did from fullback could be done even better from the libero position. He reasoned that the libero sees the field better than any other player (except, of course, the goalkeeper) and is capable of causing havoc simply by coming forward and disrupting the man-to-man marking assignments in the opponent's defense.

In the 1970 World Cup, Beckenbauer, still playing from the conventional midfield position in international competition, met with disappointment once again. He scored a crucial goal that helped the West Germans avenge their 1966 overtime loss to England in the quarter-finals, but his team was vanquished by Italy in a thrilling, but thuggish, semifinal battle. Beckenbauer bravely played the final minutes of the overtime with his arm strapped to his chest, having suffered a dislocated shoulder after being hacked down while bursting towards the Italian goal. He had been fouled just outside the penalty area, so the Germans were not rewarded with a penalty shot, and worse still, had lost the effectiveness of their leader. While technically the foul did not call for a penalty shot, "morally, it was a hundred times a penalty," wrote Glanville, adding that, in this case at least, "Crime emphatically paid, for the game was won and lost in that moment."

When the 1974 World Cup came to West Germany, Beckenbauer had a good portion of his club team on the national side. This time he was playing from his attacking libero role, having demonstrated its effectiveness by leading Bayern to a championship in the presti-

The 1974 World Cup was a memorable confrontation between West Germany and the Dutch. West German team captain Franz Beckenbauer (left) holds the Soccer World Cup together with West German goalie Sepp Maier.

gious European Champion Clubs' Cup (or the European Cup, for short).

For the 1974 World Cup, the West Germans sent a tough, unified squad that featured five of Beckenbauer's club teammates. But they didn't have an easy path to the final match. They struggled first against the Chileans, winning weakly 1-0, had a tougher-than-expected time in overcoming the brave but overmatched Australians, and lost to East Germany in a politically charged clash, the first meeting ever between the two teams. In retrospect, the embarrassing loss ended up working to the advantage of the West Germans. It "forced us to regroup. . . . We decided that if we wanted to make the final we had to work harder," said coach Helmut Schoen.

On a more basic level the loss sent them to what turned out to be the easier semifinal pool. West Germany made it to the final match by going undefeated in Group B against Poland, Sweden, and Yugoslavia. Their Eastern bloc counterparts were "rewarded" for their win by being thrown in against Argentina, Brazil, and Holland and didn't win another game in the tournament.

As many expected, the team that emerged from Group A was the Dutch. The tournament's darlings, the orange-clad, long-haired team from the Netherlands was led by that other football genius of the '70s, Johann Cruyff. The 1974 World Cup Final would be a memorable confrontation, not just between two innovative football teams but also between Franz Beckenbauer and Johann Cruyff, the world's two best players, at the peak of their games.

Born in 1947 in Amsterdam, Johann Cruyff became involved in soccer in a scenario straight out of the movies. Cruyff's father had died when Johann was just a small boy, and his mother was forced to find work as a cleaning woman for Amsterdam's Ajax (pronounced eye-YAKS) soccer club. She convinced her employers to give her son a tryout for the Ajax youth team. Johann beat out 200 other boys and made Ajax Juniors at the age of 10. Rinus Michels, the Ajax coach, remembered the scrawny Cruyff, just 5 foot 3 inches tall and 115 pounds when he was 15. "You could see that as a baby he was an exceptional player. The only obstacle was that he had no body. He learned tricks to survive."

At the age of 16, he signed to play professionally for Ajax, scored in his first match, and proceeded to lead the struggling club to six league titles, four national club championships, and three European Championships. In his nine-year career with Ajax, he scored 256 goals in 350 games. While at the time no one kept track of "assists," or goals created, the ever creative and unselfish Cruyff certainly set up hundreds more.

In 1973 Cruyff, never one to do the predictable thing, demanded a transfer to the Spanish club Barcelona, for what was then an astounding $2.25 million transfer fee. Until very recently, European soccer players were considered to be "owned" by their clubs, regardless of their contracts. When a player's contract expired, it was the club that had the option of either re-signing or "transferring" him, for sometimes astronomical sums, to another club. (The player's salary was a separate issue.) All of that was changed when a Belgian player, Jean-Marc Bosman, challenged the system. The European Court in 1995 ruled that a player in the European Union whose contract had expired could move to clubs in any other European Union country without his new club having to pay a fee.

Cruyff's performance with Barcelona eclipsed even his stellar achievements in the Dutch league, and he was dubbed *el holandes de oro,* the Golden Dutchman, for his amazing transformation of a club that had always come out second best to the teams from Madrid.

Cruyff reunited with his former Ajax coach Rinus Michels, now Barcelona's coach, on the last Sunday in October 1973. At that time, Barca was fourth from the bottom of the 18-team Spanish First Division. "From that moment," wrote Steve Englund in *Sports Illustrated*, "commenced a victory march that has not been seen since Atilla the Hun swept across Europe." Over the next five months, Barca went 26 straight games without a defeat and clinched the league championship. During the 26-game streak, Cruyff scored 16 goals and created dozens more.

In 1974, the Cruyff-led Dutch team was bringing a never-before-seen brand of soccer to the World Cup. Alluding to the Dutch team's orange uniforms and a popular movie of the day, the press called it The Clockwork Orange—but most people came to know it simply as Total Soccer. In theory, Total Soccer scrapped the whole idea of fixed positions on the field. A defender could come up to attack, and a forward could retreat to help out in defense. All players, with the exception of the goalkeeper, were meant to be completely inter-changeable. It looked like utter chaos—one writer compared it to "some drunken square dance caller . . . throwing out instructions to change partners at a faster and faster rate." Cruyff himself described it this way for Andres Cantor: "Holland does not have one style of play; it has many and applies the one appro-priate to the needs of the game . . . Every play-er knows what he has to do in every instant of the game, be it on defense, in the midfield, or on the attack. We play with total freedom, but never do we feel as free as when we are doing something to help the team."

The two best players in the world lined up against one another in front of 77,833 specta-tors in Olympic Stadium on July 7, 1974. The Dutch were the more skilled team, but their defense was suspect. In the early stages of the game, it looked as if their defensive shortcom-ings wouldn't matter a bit. Holland held onto the ball from the opening kickoff and seemed to be toying with their opponents, passing casual-ly among themselves for the first 80 seconds of the match while the Germans gave chase. No German player had even so much as touched the ball when Cruyff broke free, beat one man, made a spectacular run into the penalty area, and was brought down illegally for a penalty. Johan Neeskens converted the penalty kick, and the Dutch had the first goal before the Germans had been able to touch the ball.

Oddly, from that moment, the Dutch failed to press their advantage. West Germany, after looking hopelessly out of it, found their legs, and behind the creativity of Beckenbauer fought their way back into the match. In the

26th minute, Holland gave up a penalty—and a goal—with a foul on Bernd Holzenbein, and just before the halftime whistle, Gerd Mueller put the Germans ahead. In the second half, the Dutch launched an all-out assault on the German goal, but goalkeeper Sepp Maier and his teammates repelled shot after shot. So heavy was the Dutch pressure that at one point, Jann Jongbloed, Maier's Dutch counterpart in goal, felt comfortable enough to come 35 yards forward to play a cleared ball back into the German end with his head, an amazingly risky maneuver for a goalkeeper.

The relentless Dutch pressure created many exciting opportunities. Paul Breitner had to scramble to clear a Neeskens header off the line at the very last second, and Maier made difficult saves on hard shots from Neeskens and a header from Wim Van Hanegem. Virtually all of the action was on Germany's half of the field for the second half, but when the final whistle blew, Maier had kept the ball out of the goal for the full 89 minutes that had elapsed since the early penalty. On the surface the hero was Mueller, who scored the winner, but the all-time record holder for goals in the World Cup was always one for giving credit to his captain, Franz Beckenbauer. "I was the instrument," he once said, "for turning his genius into goals."

The West Germans had won their Cup; the Dutch were cheered enthusiastically by their fans, even in defeat, and the players took pride in a splendid effort. "There is no doubt time has shown that the 1974 World Cup had two champions," said Cruyff years later. Beckenbauer saw it differently and said, with characteristic

directness, that his team's victory was no fluke. "Had we played 10 games against Holland, we would certainly have won at least seven," he told Andres Cantor. And he was not overwhelmed by the Dutch brand of Total Soccer: "It owed more to the element of surprise than to any magic formula. I think the Dutch got away with it for so long because the opponent could not work out which tactics they were facing. It never dawned on them, certainly not until much too late, that there were no tactics at all . . . just brilliant players with a ball."

Paul Breitner of West Germany scores from the penalty spot to make the score 1-1 in the 1974 World Cup Soccer final between West Germany and Holland in Munich, West Germany.

Johann Cruyff scores the second goal for the Netherlands in the 1974 World Cup in West Germany.

That match was certainly not the last for these two great players. Cruyff, ever restless and always surprising, retired from the Dutch national team while still in his prime and refused to play in the 1978 World Cup. Then he was off to the NASL to dazzle the Americans, first for the Los Angeles Aztecs and later the Washington Diplomats. After several years in the NASL, Cruyff moved on to the world of coaching. Beginning in 1984, he coached Ajax to many years of glory. Then in 1987 he was off again to Barcelona to coach a team that he led to a European Cup championship in 1992 and four successive Spanish championships.

Beckenbauer also went to America and played alongside Pelé with the Cosmos in the late '70s. He led them to championships in 1977 and 1978, but he retired before their next win in 1982.

Beckenbauer returned to his native land and took over as coach of the West German national team in 1984. Two years later, he took his team to the final game of the World Cup in Mexico, where they lost to Argentina in a competition that was thoroughly dominated by Diego Maradona. Four years later, however, the Germans turned the tables on the South Americans and won in the final, 1–0.

Beckenbauer thus became the first man ever to win the World Cup both as captain and coach. Today he is an executive for his old club team, Bayern Munich, and his name has been featured prominently in rumors about who will succeed Joao Havelange, the president of FIFA for nearly a quarter of a century. His biggest supporter for the top job in soccer is none other than Pelé. "Franz must take the job," he said. "It would be wonderful for football and a great climax to his wonderful career."

4

"THE HAND OF GOD"

In the '80s, there would be no argument about who the best player in the world was. The Argentine media's adoring characterization of Diego Maradona as "omnipresent," "strong as a bull," "fast as a missile," and "the star of the century" was perhaps taking things a bit too far. They also said he "passed like the air through narrow spaces" and "in his veins doctors will not find blood, but rocket fuel."

But Maradona was clearly the star of world soccer—at least on the field—both as the leader of the Argentine international team and as a club player in Europe. Sadly, while Maradona's story is filled with triumphant moments, his often bizarre behavior and battles with drug abuse have obscured the fact that he was the dominant player in two successive World Cups. With his great success in the highest level of European soccer, Maradona might well have been a better player than Pelé, who was never regularly tested against the best European competition. "Pelé was the supreme player of his era; Maradona is the preeminent player of his time," stated former Argentina coach Cesar Luis Menotti. "You cannot compare them. Such greatness does not submit to comparison."

At 17, Maradona was the last player cut from the 1978 Argentina team that won the World Cup. Four years later in Spain, he played brilliantly, but like Beckenbauer before him, was

Argentina's Diego Maradona was one of soccer's preeminent players in the 1980s.

Argentine soccer superstar Diego Maradona, holding the 1986 World Cup, blows a kiss to cheering fans from the balcony of the presidential palace in Buenos Aires.

hacked out of an important match against the Italians by brutal tackling. (Unlike Beckenbauer, however, Maradona lost his cool and kicked back. He watched the end of the quarterfinal match from the sidelines, having been ejected just five minutes from the final whistle.) Twice he had missed his chance for World Cup greatness, but in Mexico in 1986 the complete Maradona—the good and bad—was on display for all the world to see.

Jere Longman of the *New York Times* wrote that, in Mexico, "Maradona fashioned the tournament into his own highlight film for the ages." Brian Glanville agreed. Mexico 1986, he wrote, "will always be remembered as Maradona's World Cup. Seldom has a player, even Pelé, so dominated the competition . . . In an era when individual talent was at a premium, defensive football more prevalent than ever, Maradona—squat, explosive, muscular, endlessly adroit—showed that a footballer of genius could still prevail."

The match most remember of that tournament—and one of the most talked-about soccer contests ever—came in the quarterfinal encounter between Argentina and England. Like the clash between West Germany and East Germany in 1974, there was more at stake than just soccer bragging rights. Four years earlier, the two nations had gone to war over the Falklands, a tiny group of islands off Argentina. "We all had cousins, fathers, nephews in the Falklands," said Argentine fullback Jose-Luis Brown, "and some of them didn't come back." The Argentines claimed the war wasn't a major motivation for them, but clearly there was some bad blood in the first soccer match between the two recent combatants.

In the days leading up to the June 22 game in Mexico City, the English team was concerned about what to do with Argentina's number 10. Defender Terry Butcher reasoned that it was impossible to come up with a special plan to stop Maradona. "You've just got to play him the way you see it on the day," he said. "You can't possibly say, do this, do that, because he can improvise, he can get out of a hole. No matter how many people are around him, he can somehow come out with the ball."

How true these words were became clear just five minutes into the second half, when Maradona scored an outrageous goal. It began like a routine play. Maradona had plowed forward into the English defense but lost the ball. Intending to pass backwards to his goalkeeper, Peter Shilton, defender Steve Hodge carelessly hooked a lazy pass over his head. Shilton came forward for the ball, but Maradona gave chase.

There seemed to be no chance in the world that Maradona could win the ball from the much taller goalkeeper, but he jumped—and suddenly the ball was in the back of the net. He had punched the ball with his hand, snapping his head back at the same time to make it appear he was heading it in. Few in the stadium were fooled—and the English team was furious—but the referee, the only man whose opinion counted, didn't have a good view and let the goal stand. After the game, when asked about his deception, Maradona rubbed salt in the wounds of the English. That goal, he said, was scored "partly by the head of Maradona, partly by the hand of God."

What happened just four minutes after the "hand of God" goal was something different altogether. Instead of Maradona the wise guy, the rule-bender, the world saw Maradona the soccer genius. One of the greatest goals ever scored started with Diego dribbling towards the English goal from his own half of the field, more than 60 yards away. He controlled the ball close to his feet while moving forward at remarkable speed. Gary Stevens came out to challenge him; Maradona swerved one way, Stevens swerved another, and was out of the play. Maradona did the same thing to Butcher. Still another defender ran straight at him, determined to take the ball or knock him down, but he came up with nothing but air. Finally, Maradona found himself alone in front of the goalkeeper. Two more players were bearing down on him at full speed, but he made them miss and then flipped the ball almost nonchalantly under Shilton who was falling down as the ball found the back of the net. Maradona had fallen to the ground himself, and the pro-Latin American crowd in Azteca Stadium roared its approval of the goal.

Afterwards, teammate Jorge Valdano said: "In that play, I trailed him because it was my job, and I ended up trailing him because of my fascination." Maradona's glorious second goal stood up as the winner. Argentina held on in the face of a furious English rally, and when the whistle blew they were on to the semifinals.

For the final against the West Germans, Maradona had created such great expectations that his performance seemed almost anti-climactic. All he did was set up the winning goal, with just six minutes to play. It was an unexpectedly difficult encounter—the final score was 3-2—but it was a win. Argentina was world champion, and no one would dispute it, especially because of the way Diego Armando Maradona had played.

At the 1990 World Cup in Italy, an injured Maradona very nearly led the undermanned Albicelestes (a nickname for the Argentine national team that refers to their striped jerseys) to a repeat World Cup championship. But this time his brilliant play was accompanied by some less than brilliant actions. Some claimed, for instance, that the Argentines were undermanned precisely because of Maradona himself, that his feud with talented center forward Ramon Diaz led to Diaz's being kept off the team. On the field, Maradona the wise guy was on display again when he used his hands in the goal area, this time to stop a score by the Soviet Union. Again he got away with it. "What a versatile player Maradona is," quipped Brazil's coach, Sebastiao Lazaroni. "He can score goals with his left hand and save them with his right."

Finally, prior to Argentina's match with Italy, Maradona foolishly appealed to Napoli fans to support Argentina—a ploy that backfired on him badly. Argentina won on penalties, but Diego had cast himself as the villain of the tournament. From then on, he was jeered every time he touched the ball.

But the old brilliance was there. Late in a crucial match against heavily favored Brazil, Maradona, playing on a severely swollen left ankle, snaked his way through the defense to feed an ingenious pass to the speedy Claudio Caniggia, who put away the game-winner. It was an amazing upset and the losers were clearly frustrated—one Brazilian player even accused the Argentine bench of handing him a bottle of drugged Gatorade.

The Argentines, plucky but short on fire-power, somehow had managed to claw their way to the final match against Germany. It was a final that most who saw it would prefer to forget. Argentina was without four players who had been suspended from previous matches, including their major goal-scoring threat Caniggia, and the tournament had taken its toll on Maradona's ankle injury. It was bad to begin with and was excruciatingly painful after six hard games. Argentina played with grim determination, Germany found countless ways not to score, and the ugly, brutal, card-filled affair was only decided when West Germany scored the lone goal, after a dubious penalty call late in the game.

Maradona was hardly a gracious loser. He refused to shake FIFA president Havelange's hand when he was given his second-place medal, and he voiced absurd conspiracy theories about "a Mafia in the soccer world" that, for reasons known only to him, wanted the Germans to beat the Argentines.

The lustre was beginning to wear off of Maradona's brilliant career. A year after Italy 1990, he failed a drug test, was investigated for links to a Naples crime ring, and was banned from football for 15 months. He refused to return to Italy. Instead he took up with Sevilla in the Spanish league but was let go for preferring night life over practice. He returned to Argentina to play for Newell's Old Boys but was again dismissed for missing training. In 1994 his strange behavior included shooting at a group of reporters with an air rifle, but he somehow put his game together enough to lead Argentina back to the World Cup. He played brilliantly in two games in USA '94, against Greece and Nigeria. But he was banned from soccer for taking a "cocktail" of performance-enhancing drugs.

Since the 1994 World Cup, Maradona's name has popped up again and again in the press, but the reports, sometimes sad, sometimes absurd, invariably have more to do with his personal life than with soccer. An Argentine magazine ran a story on a medical report that said Maradona suffered from brain damage, and that 10 years of cocaine abuse was "responsible for the odd and destructive behavior that has characterized Maradona's career." The author of the study even declared that he has not "ruled out the fear that Diego could suddenly die on a football pitch or walking down the street . . . He cannot control his aggression or detect people standing behind him." Later another physician repudiated the story, and there were reports that Maradona had successfully overcome his drug addiction in a Swiss clinic. Not long after that, however, he went on a furniture-smashing rampage after being stuck in an elevator in a Spanish hotel.

There have been signs of hope, however slim, that Maradona will get his life back on track. In late 1995, he traveled to England to be honored as "a Master Inspirer of Oxford

Argentina soccer star Diego Maradona, center, kicks his scoring shot against the Greek national team in the first round of the 1994 World Cup match.

Dreams" at Oxford University. He charmed the appreciative crowd and even came clean about the "hand of God" goal, but he was vague about when he would end his career. "I'll know [it's the end] when I no longer give people happiness."

Maradona was recently in negotiations with another Argentine club team. He would agree to play for them, he said, on two conditions: that he be allowed to redesign the team uniform, and that he not be required to practice in the morning.

SOCCER TODAY AND TOMORROW

5

There has been no clear-cut successor to Pelé, Cruyff, Beckenbauer, or Maradona in the '90s, but the decade has seen no shortage of terrific players. German goal-scoring machine Jurgen Klinsmann and midfield mastermind Matthias Sammer both deserve mention. Frenchman Eric Cantona is a highly talented, if occasionally disruptive, presence for perennial English Premier League powers Manchester United. Alan Shearer is a deadly striker both for the English national side and Newcastle United. Argentine Gabriel Batistuta is a constant danger for Fiorentina in Italy's Serie A.

Romanian Gheorghe Hagi and Bulgarian Hristo Stoichkov both made names for themselves with impressive World Cup appearances in 1990 and 1994. Dutch superstar Ruud Gullit, with his distinctive dreadlocks, was a dominant force both for his national team and for clubs PSV Eindhoven and Milan before serious knee problems shortened his playing career. Today, he is player and coach of Chelsea in the English Premier League, where he has to contend with another great Dutch striker, Dennis Bergkamp. After impressive club stints in the Netherlands and Italy, Bergkamp currently plays for Gullit's cross-London rival Arsenal.

Through the late '80s and early '90s, Italian Roberto Baggio showed promise of breaking from the pack. As a club player, he starred for

United States national team forward Eric Wynalda reacts after he scored against Switzerland in a 1994 World Cup soccer championship first-round match.

Italy's Roberto Baggio scored twice against Bulgaria in the semifinals of the 1994 World Cup.

Fiorentina from 1985 to 1990 and was then sold to Juventus of Turin, much to the dismay of Fiorentina's *tifosi,* or fans. There were riots for three days in the streets of Florence. Baggio led Juventus to the 1993 UEFA Cup and was named World Player of the Year for 1993. On the international level, he showed glimpses of brilliance in the 1990 World Cup and in the 1994 World Cup, when he almost single-handedly carried the Italian team in the final match against Brazil. After a disappointing opening round performance in which he failed score in three games and was even benched once by coach Arrigo Sacchi, Baggio got into gear in the second round, bringing his team back from the dead with clutch late goals against Nigeria and Spain, and two goals against Bulgaria in the semifinal.

No one displayed more individual brilliance than the diminutive, pony-tailed Baggio in that World Cup, but sadly, he will be remembered most for blasting the ball over the crossbar when it was his turn to take a penalty shot in the end-game shoot-out against Brazil. "It's been nearly two years, and I still have nightmares about that missed shot," he told Brazilian journalists in June 1996. The following year he was a substitute for AC Milan and was not happy about it. "At the moment I feel like a Ferrari being driven by a traffic warden," he said regarding his under-utilization by Milan coach Arrigo Sacchi (the same man who benched him in the World Cup).

Paolo Maldini, one of Baggio's teammates at Milan, could well be remembered as one of the all-time great players by the time he retires, but that's still a long way off. He's hindered slightly in terms of recognition by the fact that he's a defender, a left back, but that's about all he has going against him. In his favor are movie-star good looks, an amazing string of more than 70 international appearances (he's still only 28), and the fact that his father, Cesare Maldini, is the successor to Sacchi as the coach of the Italian national team. Maldini is one of the most highly regarded players in the world. Prior to the 1996 European Championships in England, *World Soccer* magazine called him "the greatest player in [the tournament] by a mile." He has been instrumental in leading Milan to the *scudetto* (or "badge," a term for the Italian league championship) in 1988, 1992, 1993, and 1994. He led

Milan to the European Champions' Cup in 1989, 1990, and 1994 and took Italy to their high finishes in the 1990 and 1994 World Cup appearances.

When Maldini was named World Player of the Year for 1994, it marked the first time the award has ever gone to a defender. He accepted the award on behalf of all defenders, characterizing it as "a particular matter of pride because defenders generally receive so much less attention from fans and the media than goal scorers." He went on to credit all the training his father had given him as a boy. The elder Maldini was also a great player for Milan and Italy and coached the Italian under-21 squad before being named coach of the senior team.

While Brazil was a powerful force and deserving champion of the 1994 World Cup, one can only wonder what their team would have been like had they unleashed a young player who now, at the age of 21, inspires comparisons to Pelé as much for the joy he brings to the game as for his skill in scoring goals. Ronaldo, a powerfully built center-forward who plays, with his head shaved, for Barcelona, has been compared to a "steam-roller and computer-generated Ferrari engine programmed to score," in the words of a rival Spanish league coach. Andoni Zubizarreta, the goalkeeper for the Spanish national team, said what he found most impressive about Ronaldo's game was "his ability to pick up the ball in no man's land, when there is simply nothing on, and turn that into a goal-scoring situation all on his own."

Johann Cruyff, Ronaldo's coach at Barcelona until early 1997, sounded a cautionary note. "All the praise," he said, is "exaggerated" and "not good for Ronaldo" because it puts too much pressure on him. Pelé loves what he sees in his reputed successor but agrees with Cruyff that all the hype might have an adverse effect on the young superstar. Calling him "an exquisite footballer who lives to score goals," Pelé nevertheless warns that it's not "doing him any favors comparing him to me all the time."

How does Ronaldo see himself? Apparently all the success is not going to his head. He grew up in intense poverty, learning to play in the garbage dumps of Rio de Janeiro. Legend has it that his inability to come up with the bus fare was all that kept him from making the Flamengo club team at an early age. Perhaps because of his early struggles, Ronaldo has retained a refreshing modesty: "I'm flattered that people think I'm good. But I'm only just getting started." He has taken a strong stance on clean living ("Drugs are out—training is in") and sees himself as owing something to his fans instead of the other way around. "I don't mind signing autographs, but what I really want to do is give the fans a lot of goals."

One of the most interesting questions for soccer as it approaches the 21st century concerns the game's development in America. Will the hosting of the 1994 World Cup, a fledgling professional league, and an always-improving national team make soccer the major sport its fans think it should be? The proper attitude at this point appears to be one of cautious opti-

United States soccer player Tab Ramos (9) runs past Brazil's Dunga during the second round of the 1994 World Cup Soccer match. In the background watching the action is Fernando Clavijo of the United States.

mism. Soccer could succeed here if Major League Soccer (MLS) continues to improve on its better-than-expected popularity in its first season (the projections for overall attendance were exceeded by a full 50 percent). The sport will take off if the U.S. team qualifies for, and performs well in, the 1998 World Cup in France and if American-bred players continue to excel, both in MLS and in foreign leagues.

MLS has already shown that growing pains might be a problem. The quality of play may be somewhat uneven; many of the marquee American players and some foreign stars will miss games in 1998 because they have to play with their national teams in World Cup qualifying games. There has been controversy—and a class-action lawsuit by some players—regarding the league's rigidly centralized structure. MLS's main office controls every aspect of the league's business, even matters that are traditionally handled by the individual clubs. The main office says which players play on which teams and how much each player will be paid. For most, that's not very much. The maximum MLS salary is less than the minimum salary in the National Basketball Association.

The good news for the league is that many of the best Americans are giving up bigger salaries to play at home. Striker Eric Wynalda earned more than $2 million in his three years playing for FC Saarbrucken in the Bundesliga but is happy to be playing for less for the San Jose Clash. "I'd rather make $250,000 here than $1 million in Germany," he told *Sports Illustrated*. The greatest goal-scorer ever for the U.S. national team, Wynalda was not just a curiosity playing overseas. He was a legitimate star—he scored nine goals in his first 10 games and was the constant focus of gossip and media scrutiny in Germany.

Similarly, midfielder Tab Ramos played five seasons in Spain for Real Betis, then played in the Mexican First Division before coming home to the MetroStars, a team that plays close to Tab's hometown of Kearney, New Jersey—the same hometown, incidentally, that produced former U.S. goalkeeper Tony Meola and current national team captain John Harkes.

Alexi Lalas, the first American-born player ever to compete in Italy's Serie A, is another U.S. star who prefers playing in his native land over playing overseas. In two seasons with Padova, he gained the respect of players in the best league in the world and scored the winning goal for his side against both AC Milan and Inter Milan during the 1994-95 season. For the past two years he's been back in the

U.S. player Alexi Lalas, back to camera, falls to the ground fighting for control of the ball during the United States vs. Switzerland World Cup soccer championship first round match.

States, playing for the New England Revolution and, of course, the U.S. national team. "For a lot of us," he told an interviewer for the on-line magazine *Soccer Ink*, "for many, many years we've been talking about being able to come back to the United States and play in front of family and friends and also make a good living. And for a lot of us, we didn't think that time would ever come . . . So when the opportunity came about, most of us jumped at the chance.

"I think that's evident by the number of players that decided to forego their careers overseas and come back to work, because we are giving up money, and we're making sacrifices just like everybody else is," he continued. "But it's much more important to the growth of soccer and the future of soccer [to have the best U.S. players competing in America]. I think most of us have a commitment, and we feel a responsibility to help promote the game and continue what [was] started many, many years ago before I was even involved."

John Harkes is yet another American who played well for an overseas club, Sheffield Wednesday of the English Premier League. He recalls the struggle for acceptance in England was a difficult one. "The hardest thing was being accepted as an American," he told Pete Davies. "Everybody's going, why should we let him play here, he's taking a job off someone else—so I had to play twice as well as anybody, every single day." But his struggle was worth it. In 1993, he became the first American to score a goal in a match at London's hallowed Wembley Stadium. Today Harkes is a star for D.C. United and, while he won't rule out the possibility of playing for another overseas club team, one thing is certain. He will be a fixture in midfield for the United States team for years to come. Coach Steve Sampson thinks so highly of his talent and leadership that he named Harkes U.S. team captain for as long as he plays.

Not all of the best American players have come home to roost, however. Ernie Stewart, a star in the 1994 World Cup, still plays in the Netherlands. Claudio Reyna, a young, gifted midfielder who missed the entire 1994 World Cup with a torn hamstring, plays for Bayer Leverkusen in Germany, alongside veteran American national team member Thomas Dooley. And Kasey Keller, the probable starting U.S. goalkeeper, has been overseas since 1992, getting valuable experience and gaining a good international reputation playing with Millwall, a team in England's First Division. In late 1996, Keller, who was well-liked by fans and teammates alike at Millwall (he was voted the team MVP in 1993), was transferred to Leicester City of the English Premier League, becoming only the second American goalie to play at the highest level in England. Juergen Sommer, his U.S. team backup, was the first.

The American squad has performed well, if not brilliantly, in their World Cup qualifying. Barring a major collapse, they should be one of the three teams to make it from their region. Keller, in an on-line chat session at the Soccer America World Wide Web site, described the team's blend of raw talent and experience. "The strength we have right now is that we have a very good core of players and an influx of youth players. In past qualifying periods, it's seemed that the youth coming in was better

The American squad made a good showing in the 1994 World Cup competition. The current team's blend of talent and experience makes them "well worth watching."

than the experienced players, so we were always fielding a team with no experience. Now there are a lot of players who've been in Europe, who've got a World Cup or two under their belt, and we've got a good combination of youth and experience."

The most recent ranking by FIFA had the U.S. team the 22nd best team in the world, but not long before that they were ranked as high as number 16. If that poll means anything, it means the Americans are not quite at the top level but not too far behind it either. At one point in late 1996, they were attempting to win their third consecutive World Cup qualifying match, which moved Michael Bamberger, a *Sports Illustrated* writer, to comment, "There was a time, not so long ago, that the thought of the U.S. winning three straight World Cup qualifying matches would have been absurd." But it's no longer far-fetched at all. As Eric Wynalda told Bamberger, "People may not realize it yet, but we're a very good, very experienced team."

They are well worth watching.

FURTHER READING

Cantor, Andres, with Daniel Arcucci. *GOOOAL! A Celebration of Soccer.* New York: Simon & Schuster, 1996.

Davies, Pete. *Twenty-Two Foreigners in Funny Shorts: The Intelligent Fan's Guide to Soccer and World Cup '94.* New York: Random House, 1994.

Glanville, Brian. *The Story of the World Cup.* London: Faber and Faber, 1993.

Gardner, Paul. *The Simplest Game: The Intelligent Fan's Guide to the World of Soccer.* New York: Collier Books, 1994.

Radnedge, Keir, general editor. *The Ultimate Encyclopedia of Soccer: The Definitive Illustrated Guide to World Soccer.* Rocklin, California: Prima Publishing, 1994.

ABOUT THE AUTHOR

Tim Ungs is the author of *Shaquille O'Neal* in Chelsea House's Basketball Legends series. A native of Minneapolis, Minnesota, he received English degrees from the University of Notre Dame (B.A.) and the University of Minnesota (M.A.). A freelance writer, he has been a reviewer and editor for the Excite online service, and before that he worked at HarperCollins Publishers in New York for five years—most recently as an in-house copywriter for the Adult Trade Division. He lives in Brooklyn, New York, with his wife and dog.

INDEX

PICTURE CREDITS   AP/Wide World Photos: pp. 2, 6, 9, 10, 15, 18, 20, 26, 27, 28, 29, 30, 33, 39, 40, 42, 44, 50, 52, 54, 58, 59, 62